MYSTERY MATH
A FIRST BOOK OF ALGEBRA

by David A. Adler • illustrated by Edward Miller

Holiday House / New York

If you've ever been on a seesaw,
you know something about equations.
You know something about algebra.

A seesaw is like an equation.
A seesaw must be balanced.
An equation must be balanced too.
Whatever is on one side should be
balanced by whatever is on the other side.

If a small pumpkin is placed
on one side of a seesaw,
someone or something small
should be on the other side.

If a large pumpkin is placed on one side, someone or something heavy should be on the other side.

An **EQUATION** is a sentence
with an **EQUAL SIGN (=)**.

An equation must be balanced.

This is an equation:

$$4 + 1 = 3 + 2.$$

Each side of the = adds up to 5.

The two sides are balanced.
They're equal.

No Trespassing!

Here are some more equations:

6 + 2 = 8,

5 − 1 = 3 + 1,

4 + 1 = 5.

The two sides of each equation are balanced.

They're equal.

Keep Out!

An **ALGEBRA EQUATION**
has an equal sign and an unknown,
a **MYSTERY NUMBER**.

Here's an algebra equation:

$$4 + X = 5.$$

represents the unknown,
the mystery number.

Since 4 + X = 5 is an equation,
we know that whatever is on
one side of the = must be equal to
whatever is on the other side.
4 + X = 5 is an easy mystery to solve.

4 + what number
would equal 5?

$$4 + 1 = 5$$

In the equation

$$4 + X = 5,$$

the X (the unknown, the mystery number)
is 1.

In the equation

$$Y + 1 = 7,$$

Y represents the unknown,
the mystery number.
What is the value of Y?
The value of Y is 6.

In the equation

$$3 - Z = 1,$$

what is the value of Z?

The value of Z is 2.

The unknown, or mystery number,
in algebra is also called the

VARIABLE because the value of

$X, Y, Z,$ or whatever letter or symbol is
used, varies from one equation to the next.

Once you know how to find the mystery number, the variable, in an algebra equation, you can use algebra to solve word problems.

Sometimes you can just look at a word problem and know the answer.

Sometimes you can just look at an algebra equation and know what the mystery number is. But sometimes you have to add, subtract, multiply, or divide to find the variable, the mystery number.

Haunted House Ahead

KEEP OUT!

The simple rule is: whatever is done to one side of the equal sign must be done to the other side.

ADDITION can help you solve word problems and algebra equations.

Mandy and Billy stopped by a large, creepy haunted house. Lots of ravens were on the telephone wires beside the house.

"Caw caw," the ravens called, and then one by one they flew away.

"I saw 6 birds fly away," Mandy told Billy. "Then I counted 13 birds still on the wires!"

How many birds were on the wires when Mandy and Billy first stopped by the creepy haunted house?

Mandy and Billy's problem can be
written as an algebra equation.

Let R be the number of ravens on the wires
when Mandy and Billy stopped by the house.

R – the 6 ravens that flew off
= the 13 ravens still on the wires.

$$R - 6 = 13$$

To find the value of R,
you want to get it alone on
one side of the equal sign.
What must you do to get R alone?
You must elimate the – 6.
You can do that by adding 6 to
each side of the equation.

$$R - 6 = 13$$
$$+\ 6 \quad +\ 6$$
$$\overline{019}$$

$$R + 0 = 19$$

$$R = 19$$

There were 19 ravens on the telephone wires when
Mandy and Billy first stopped by the house.

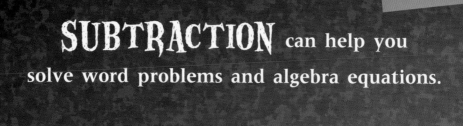

SUBTRACTION can help you
solve word problems and algebra equations.

Igor is the caretaker of the haunted house.
He told Mandy and Billy, "There were bats flying
around in here before I started my lunch. Then
while I ate my lunch I saw 12 more bats fly in.
Now there are 27 in the house."
How many were in the house before lunch?

The caretaker's problem can be
written as an algebra equation.

Let Y be the number of bats in
the haunted house before lunch.

Y + the 12 bats that went in at lunchtime
= the 27 bats in there now.

$$Y + 12 = 27$$

To find the value of Y, you want to get
it alone on one side of the equal sign.
What must you do to get Y alone?
You must eliminate the + 12.
You can do that by subtracting 12
from each side of the equation.

$$Y + 12 = 27$$
$$\underline{-\ 12} \quad \underline{-\ 12}$$
$$0 \quad\quad 15$$

$$Y + 0 = 15$$

$$Y = 15$$

Before lunch there were 15
bats in the haunted house.

MULTIPLICATION

can help you solve word
problems and algebra equations.

"Yikes!" Billy said when he
and Mandy left the house.
"I'm glad to get out of there.
Skeletons were everywhere."
Mandy asked Igor, "How many
skeletons are in the house?"
"I won't tell you," Igor said, and laughed.
"But I'll give you an algebra problem.
Solve the problem and you'll know
how many skeletons there are."
Billy took a pen and notebook
from his backpack.
"Take our mystery number (the number
of skeletons in the house) and divide
that by 4 (the number of rooms in the
house), and you'll get 5 (the number
of skeletons in each room."

Here's what Billy wrote: $\dfrac{Z}{4} = 5$

Z is the number of skeletons in the haunted house.

4 is the number of rooms in the house.

5 is the number of skeletons in each room.

In the equation $\dfrac{Z}{4} = 5$, $\dfrac{Z}{4}$ means that Z is divided by 4.

To find the value of Z, you want to get it alone on one side of the equal sign. You can do that by multiplying each side of the equation by 4.

$\dfrac{Z}{4}$ multiplied by 4 = 5 multiplied by 4

Z multiplied by 4 is $4Z$, so . . .

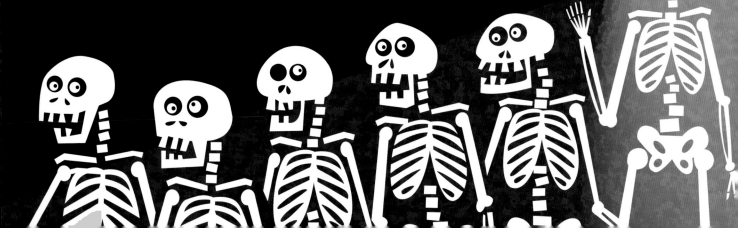

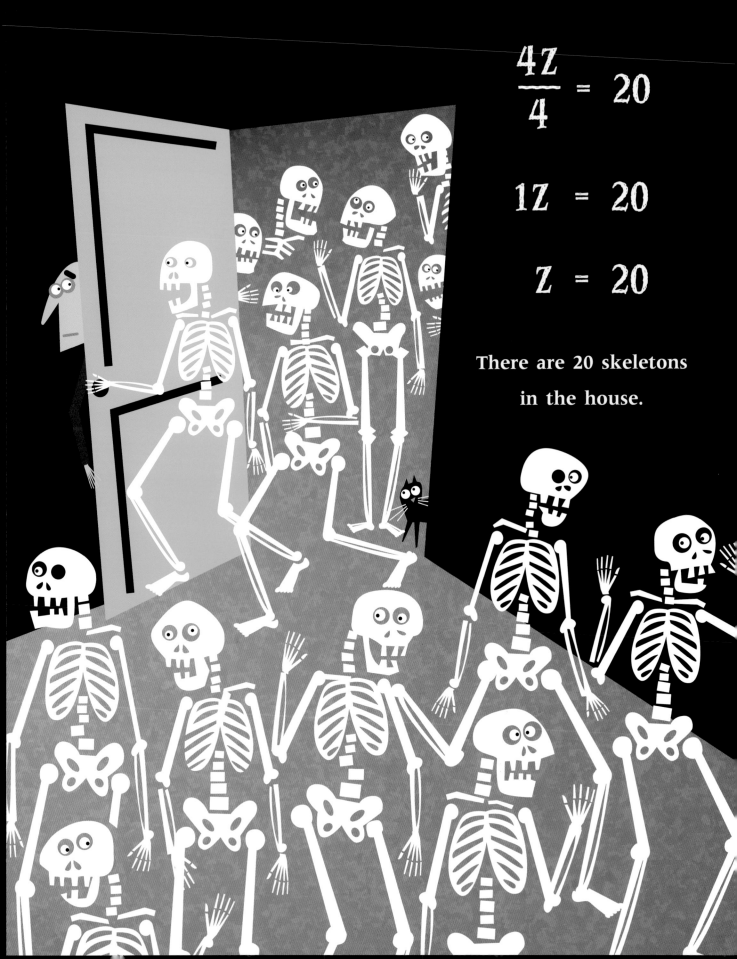

$$\frac{4Z}{4} = 20$$

$$1Z = 20$$

$$Z = 20$$

There are 20 skeletons
in the house.

DIVISION can help you solve
word problems and algebra equations.
Igor told Mandy and Billy, "I have a black cat,
and my cat had kittens. I won't tell you how
many kittens I have, but I will tell you
that the kittens have 28 legs total."
How many kittens does Igor have?

Let K be the number of kittens.

Since each kitten has 4 legs,

4 multiplied by K = 28.

$$4K = 28$$

The equation $4K = 28$ means

4 multiplied by K equals 28.
To find the value of K, you want to get it alone
on one side of the equal sign. You can do that
by dividing each side of the equation by 4.

4 multiplied by K divided by $4 = 28$ divided by 4

$$\frac{4K}{4} = \frac{28}{4}$$

$$1K = 7$$

$$K = 7$$

Igor's cat had 7 kittens.

You already know how to add, subtract,
multiply, and divide.
Now you know how that helps
you with algebra.
Solving mysteries is fun!
Algebra helps you solve
math mysteries.

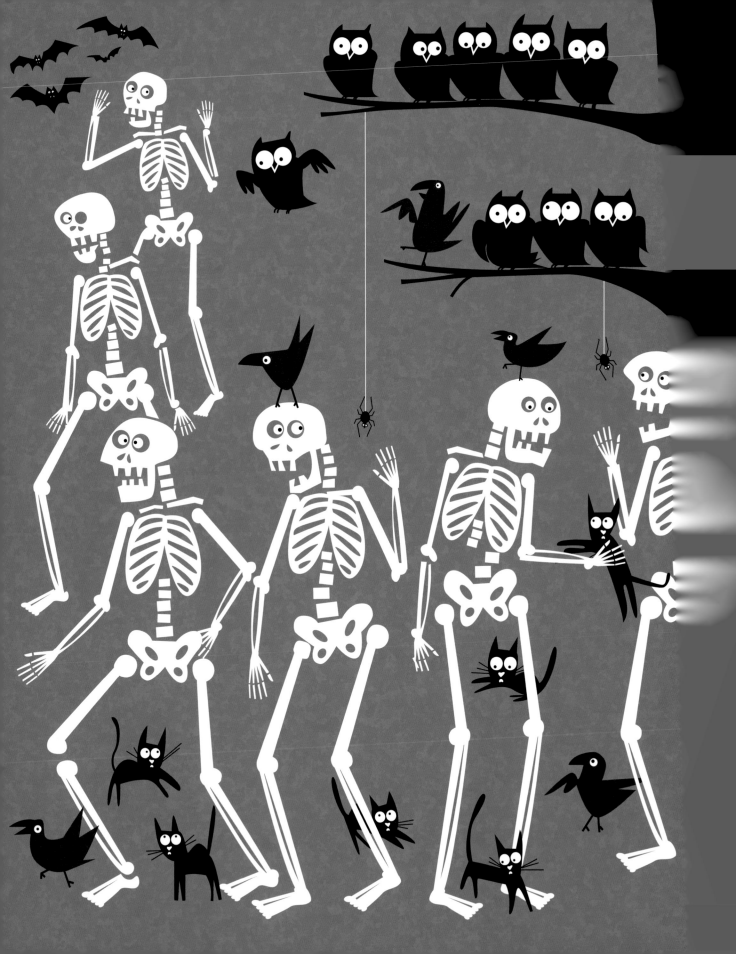

FUN WITH ALGEBRA:
LET'S MAKE A BALANCE SCALE

Many years ago small items were weighed on balance scales. Balance scales are like equations. When the scale is in balance, the weight on one side of the scale equals the weight on the other side.

To make your balance scale, you will need:

- 40 pennies
- masking tape
- a pair of scissors
- a hole puncher
- a fine point marker
- 2 large paper clips
- a wire hanger
- an adult to supervise

You can make weights and your own balance scale, then use them to play with algebra and find the unknown number in an equation.

To make your weights, make two piles each of two pennies, four pennies, six pennies, and eight pennies. As in the drawing, wrap each pile of pennies with about two inches of tape. Fold the tape over. With the hole puncher, make a hole in one end of the tape. With the fine point marker, mark each weight with the number of pennies inside.

To make your balance scale, bend open two large paper clips until each forms a large S.

Hook the hanger over a clothes rod so it hangs free.

You now have weights and a balance scale.

It's important that the clips be at the very ends of the hanger. Use two small pieces of masking tape to keep the paper clips in place. Test your scale. Hang a four-penny weight on one side. Hang two of the two-penny weights on the other side. The two sides should balance.

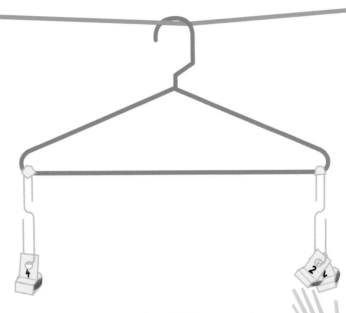

Now use your balance scale to solve this algebra equation:

$$8 = 2 + X$$

Hang an eight-penny weight on the left side of the scale. Hang a two-penny weight on the right side. The left side should be hanging lower than the right side. The scale is not balanced.

Try hanging different weights on the right side. Which weight added to the right side balances the scale? What is the value of X?

Now use your scale to solve these equations:

$$8 = 6 + X$$

$$2 + Y = 4$$

$$6 + Z = 8 + 2$$

$$X + 8 = 6 + 4$$

FOR MY FAVORITE MATH TEACHER,
MY BROTHER JOE —D. A. A.

TO MATH TEACHERS —E. M.

The publisher would like to thank Grace Wilkie for reviewing this book for accuracy. Grace is the past president of the Association of Mathematics Teachers of New York State and New York State Mathematics Honor Society as well as an expert on Common Core Standards, National Council of Teachers of Mathematics Standards, and New York State Mathematics Standards.

Library of Congress Cataloging-in-Publication Data

Adler, David A.
Mystery math : a first book of algebra / by David A. Adler ;
illustrated by Edward Miller.
p. cm.
ISBN 978-0-8234-2289-0 (hardcover)
1. Algebra—Juvenile literature. I. Miller, Edward, 1964- II. Title.
QA155.15.M55 2011
512—dc22
2010024188

Visit www.davidaadler.com for more information on the author, for a list of his books, and to download teacher's guides and educational materials. You can also learn more about the writing process, take fun quizzes, and read select pages from David A. Adler's books.

Edward Miller is a former children's book art director. He illustrates a variety of products for kids in addition to books. Follow him on Instagram @edelementary.